MW01129105

TRAVELING IN NEW YORK CITY

ANDREW MOORE

Rosen
Classroom.

New York is always busy with people
moving from place to place! People in New
York City can choose from many kinds of
transportation.

Some people walk to school, work, or to the store every day. Walking is **healthy** and helps keep people strong.

Other people ride bicycles, or even skateboards, to go from place to place. Some New York City streets have special **bicycle lanes** to keep people on bicycles safe.

To go longer distances, sometimes people take a bus. Buses go almost everywhere in New York City. They are driven by bus **drivers**. Have you ever taken a bus?

This yellow car is called a **taxi.** A taxi is driven
by a taxi driver. The taxi driver knows the
names of all the city streets and how to get
anywhere.

Subways are trains that run mostly underground. To ride the subway, people must enter a **subway station**. The stations are often beneath the city streets.

The subway is a fast way to travel from one place in the city to another. The subway map helps people know what streets are above them. A subway train can be 600 feet long! It can have 11 cars.

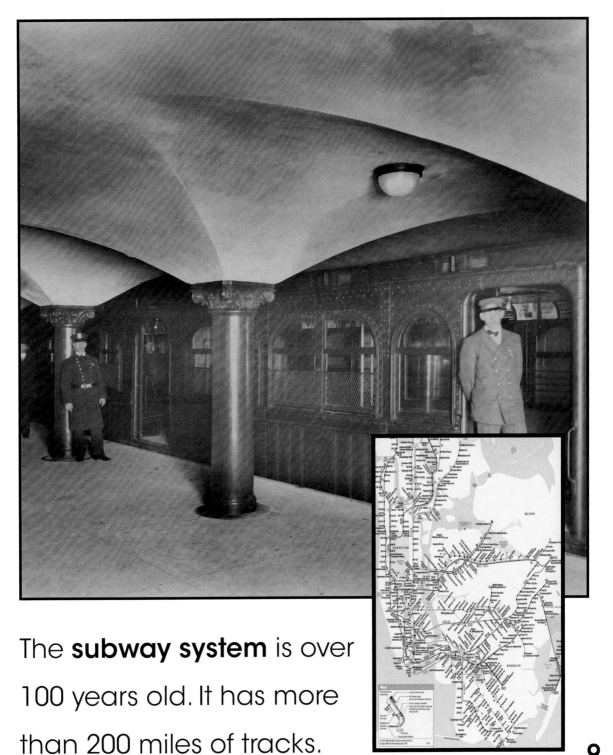

The **subway system** is over 100 years old. It has more than 200 miles of tracks.

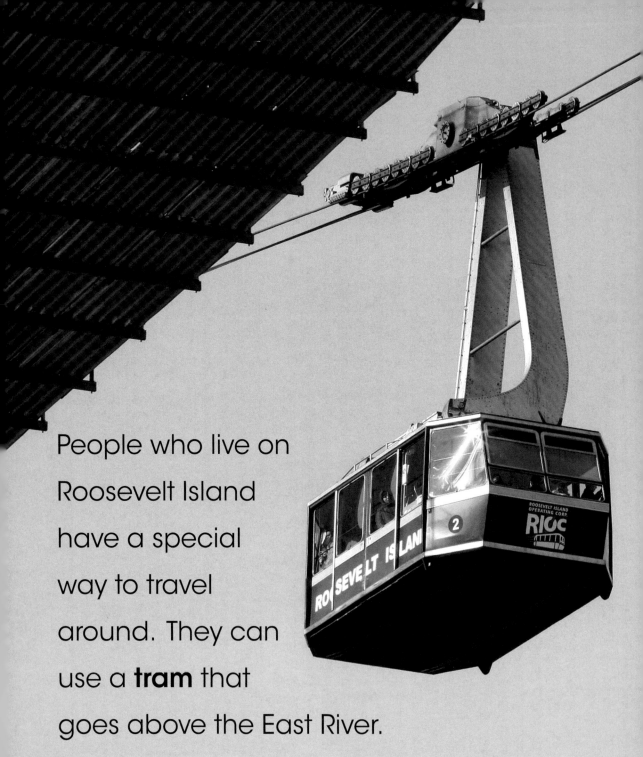

People who live on
Roosevelt Island
have a special
way to travel
around. They can
use a **tram** that
goes above the East River.

Some people take a **ferry** to go to work and to go home. The Staten Island Ferry takes people from the borough of Staten Island to the borough of Manhattan. In New York City, there are so many ways to travel from place to place!

Glossary

bicycle lanes: special places in the streets for people to ride their bikes

drivers: people who drive cars, buses, or trucks

ferry: a boat that goes back and forth between two places

healthy: in good condition

subways: trains that often go under the ground

subway station: a place where you get on and off the subway

subway system: all the railways for the subway

taxi: a car with a driver whom you pay to take you a short distance

tram: a small car above the ground that travels on a cable

transportation: a way to carry people or things from one place to another